TOOLS FOR CAREGIVERS

- **F&P LEVEL:** C
- **WORD COUNT:** 27
- **CURRICULUM CONNECTIONS:** animals, habitats, nature

Skills to Teach

- **HIGH-FREQUENCY WORDS:** a, for, it(s), see, they, up
- **CONTENT WORDS:** air, comes, dolphin(s), eats, fish, flippers, jumps, play, swim(s), tail, teeth
- **PUNCTUATION:** exclamation point, periods, questions marks
- **WORD STUDY:** digraph *ph* (*dolphin*); long /a/, spelled *ai* (*air, tail*); long /a/, spelled *ay* (*play*); long /e/, spelled *ea* (*eats*); long /e/, spelled *ee* (*see, teeth*)
- **TEXT TYPE:** information report

Before Reading Activities

- Read the title and give a simple statement of the main idea.
- Have students "walk" through the book and talk about what they see in the pictures.
- Introduce new vocabulary by having students predict the first letter and locate the word in the text.
- Discuss any unfamiliar concepts that are in the text.

After Reading Activities

Explain to readers that the "ph" in "dolphins" is a digraph. A digraph is two letters put together to make a combined sound. The digraph "ph" makes an /f/ sound. "Phone" is another example. "Th" is a common digraph, such as the "th" in "the." Ask readers to name words that use the diagraph "ph" or "th." Write their answers on the board.

Tadpole Books are published by Jump!, 5357 Penn Avenue South, Minneapolis, MN 55419, www.jumplibrary.com

Copyright ©2024 Jump!. International copyright reserved in all countries. No part of this book may be reproduced in any form without written permission from the publisher.

Editor: Jenna Gleisner **Designer:** Emma Almgren-Bersie

Photo Credits: Ricardo Canino/Shutterstock, cover; BearFotos/Shutterstock, 1; pukach/Shutterstock, 2tl, 2bl, 8–9; slowmotiongli/Shutterstock, 2tr, 3; georgeclerk/iStock, 2ml, 14–15; yeshaya dinerstein/Shutterstock, 2mr, 4–5; David Jefferson/Alamy, 2br, 10–11; Jamen Percy/Shutterstock, 6–7; PaulVinten/iStock, 12–13; MattiaATH/iStock, 16.

Library of Congress Cataloging-in-Publication Data
Names: Deniston, Natalie, author.
Title: Dolphins / by Natalie Deniston.
Description: Minneapolis, MN: Jump!, Inc., [2024]
Series: My first animal books | Includes index.
Audience: Ages 3–6
Identifiers: LCCN 2023020979 (print)
LCCN 2023020980 (ebook)
ISBN 9798885246583 (hardcover)
ISBN 9798885246590 (paperback)
ISBN 9798885246606 (ebook)
Subjects: LCSH: Dolphins—Juvenile literature.
Classification: LCC QL737.C432 D47 2024 (print)
LCC QL737.C432 (ebook)
DDC 599.53—dc23/eng/20230512
LC record available at https://lccn.loc.gov/2023020979
LC ebook record available at https://lccn.loc.gov/2023020980

MY FIRST ANIMAL BOOKS

DOLPHINS

by Natalie Deniston

TABLE OF CONTENTS

Words to Know..........................2

Dolphins................................3

Let's Review!...........................16

Index..................................16

WORDS TO KNOW

flippers

jumps

play

swims

tail

teeth

DOLPHINS

A dolphin jumps.

It swims.

tail

See its tail?

flipper

See its flippers?

See its teeth?

Dolphins swim.

They play!

LET'S REVIEW!

Dolphins swim and live in the ocean. What body parts help them swim? Name and point to them.

INDEX

air 7
eats 11
flippers 9
jumps 3

play 15
swims 5, 13
tail 8
teeth 10